# SURVIVING DESTRUCTION AS A HUMAN BEING

Robert E. Daley

The Larry Czerwonka Company, LLC
Hilo, Hawai'i

First Edition — December 2015

This book is set in 14-point Garamond

Published by: The Larry Czerwonka Company, LLC
czerwonkapublishing.com

Printed in the United States of America

ISBN: 0692600396
ISBN-13: 978-0692600399

All scriptures used in this work are taken from the
King James Version of the Scriptures.

BOOKS BY **ROBERT E. DALEY**

A Case for "Threes"
A Simple Plan . . . of Immense Complexity
Armour, Weapons, And Warfare
from Everlasting to Everlasting
Killer Sex
Life or Death, Heaven or Hell, You Choose!
Raptures and Resurrections
Short Tales
So . . . What Happens to the Package?
Study and Interpretation of The Scriptures Made Simple
Surviving Destruction as A Human Being
The Gospel of John
The Gospel of John (Red Edition)
The League of The Immortals
The New Testament - Pauline Revelation
The New Testament - Pauline Revelation Companion
"The World That Then Was . . ." & The Genesis That Now Is
What Color Are You?
What Makes A Christian Flaky?
What Really Happened to Judas Iscariot?
Who YOU Are in Christ . . . RIGHT NOW!

## The Enhancement Series

#1 Book of Ecclesiastes
#2 Book of Daniel
#3 Book of Romans
#4 Book of Galatians
#5 Book of Hebrews

## The Deeper Things of God Series

#1 The Personage of God
#2 The Personage of Man
#3 The Personage of Christ

# Introduction

**DISCLAIMER:** So that **YOU** will be able to put down this little exposé work right now, before it burns your tender fingertips, and not be compelled to have to go any further, please be advised . . . we are going to be talking about the real Person of GOD, the written Word of God, and both Spiritual and Physical Life and Death Realities.

Should **YOU** be able to successfully, personally, avoid the reality of physical DEATH . . . whether now or later . . . then the material contained within this little work is *Not* necessarily for **YOU**.

Should **YOU** currently be so terrified of hearing the truth about spiritual realities of Life and Death, because much sooner than later your own personal misconceptions and falsehoods will be stripped nakedly away and exposed before your very eyes, then this little work is *Not* necessarily for **YOU**.

## HOWEVER . . . please be advised . . .

**YOU** are a HUMAN BEING . . . and there is nothing that **YOU** can do about that, so there is no escape from what is presented within these pages.

**YOU** are, most likely, dead in your vile and ugly sins and probably do not even know about the Spiritual Realm and about Spiritual Life and Death issues.

**YOU** will almost certainly physically die at some future point in time . . . and when **YOU** do, that fantasy-bubble that you are currently living within will suddenly burst, and **YOU** will be faced with the spiritual realities of the Life and Death issues that govern this entire universe. **YOU** will then suddenly believe in that which **YOU** currently ignore, and have chosen to *Not* believe in right now . . . but it will all be too late. Spiritual, mental, emotional, and physical **DESTRUCTION** will await **YOU**.

The spiritual reality is that **GOD** declares in His Word that He *"is not slack concerning his promise, as some men count slackness; but is longsuffering to us-ward, not willing that any should perish, but that all should come to repentance."* (II Peter 3:9)

But sadly most people are unaware of that truth, and so people, in general, are ultimately going to do, what people will normally do, regardless of God's attempt to rescue them.

∗ ∗ ∗

Why is it that people are so resistant to hearing the Truth? Are **YOU** resistant?

Do people really believe that this life is just one big exciting game? Some sort of designed *Circle of Life* like

Walt Disney purports? Do **YOU** believe that this life is only a game?—Who put Walt Disney in charge anyway?

Do people really believe that there is no right or wrong? And that there is never going to be any requirement of accountability? That everyone that thinks that they are a *nice person* is going to go to Heaven when they die? That only *wicked people,* such as the evil person in the movie "Ghost", ultimately go to Hell? Do **YOU** believe that nonsense?

Do Liars get to go to Heaven when they die . . . ? Who says that they do? Or doesn't it really matter if **YOU** are a liar?

Do Fornicators get to go to Heaven when they die . . . ? Who says that they do? Or doesn't it really matter if **YOU** are sexually liberal, because sexually, moral, behavior is only a matter of Social acceptance?

Do Homosexuals get to go to Heaven when they die . . . ? Who says that they do? Or is sexual *lifestyle* behavior simply dependent upon Societal acceptance? Who put the prevailing Society in charge anyway?

Do Drug Addicts get to go to Heaven when they die . . . ? Who says that they do? Or is deceptively-destructive, self-abusive, corrosive behavior just a matter of personal choice?

Is **The Judgment Day** really going to be a real *Day?* Or have religious people simply made that *Day* up to scare us?

Do only the *Bad* and *Wicked* people have to go to Hell when they die? . . . Who is it that says that any-way, the *Nice* people?

Do all of the *Nice* people in the world automatically get to go to Heaven when they die? . . . Who is it that says that they do, the other *Nice* people? Who put the *Nice* people in charge anyway?

Who really says whether a person is *Naughty* or *Nice* to begin with? Santa Claus?

# Where Is The Creator God or His Word Within This Picture?

# Foundational Premise

#1.  The fallacy, of the notion of *The Evolution of Man*, is a genuine myth fabricated by men and comes straight from the Pit of Hell . . . and . . . the reality, of *Original Creation by God* concerning all things, is the actual reality that comes from the Spirit of Truth.

#2.  HUMAN BEINGS . . . did not originate as swamp slime, or amoebas, or fish, or lizards, or monkeys, or any other kind of creature that innately belongs to the complimentary Animal Kingdom.

#3.  HUMAN BEINGS . . . did not *evolve* in the past, and are not *evolving* in the present, in any aspect . . . and are not right now on the top-shelf of candidates and the highest creature of the animal compliment *food-chain*.

#4.  HUMAN BEINGS . . . were never any kind of prehistoric *cavemen* that eked out their existence and livelihood by bludgeoning to death the animal compliment that was all around them, and were able to continue because of the survival of the fittest.

Reprobate, sin-saturated, God-hating, two-dimensional thinking men, have put forth their postulations of occurrences, within the corridors of *time*, based on faulty *scientific* evidence, that has been custom tailored to fit their own particular wicked beliefs and evil agendas.

# Use Your Brain!

Does a God of ordered Creation really exist . . . or does He not? **Or** maybe this extremely complex universe is simply a Godless void that somehow *just happened* on its own from the explosion of a Big Bang? Boom!

Is there really an unseen enemy known of as the Devil . . . whose actual name is Satan . . . or is there not? **Or** is he merely an animated fictional character created by Stan Lee and MARVEL comics?

Do readily known Demon entities really exist . . . or do they not? **Or** are all of the demon-possessed people of this world simply medically *bi-polar* or *schizophrenic*?

Is there really an active, functioning, invisible world that we cannot see . . . or is there not? **Or** are we all deluded, and the multitude of all of the established evidence that we have for the existence of that world, just simply fabricated?

Is the certainty of physical DEATH something that is really real . . . or is it not? **Or** do we simply go to the funerals of friends and family just to get some free food?

Was Jesus Christ of Nazareth, a real historical person who walked upon this Earth . . . or was he not? **Or** is he only the *figment* of millions of people's imaginations?

For two-thousand years this world has hated the Jewish people, and they have been stigmatized and labeled as the "Christ Killers" . . . is that true or false?

In these last days that we are living in right now, the world is rapidly moving toward a hatred of genuine Christian people, because genuine Christians choose to believe the Bible, and purpose to live in a godly manner . . . is that true or false?

Are you really sure that you are a real person . . . or possibly not? **Or** are you simply a blow-up fabricated facsimile that chooses to spew out vulgarity, think foul thoughts, and behave in a reprobate manner?

To all of the questions hence posed . . . Get a Grip!

\* \* \*

*We are going to purpose to reference the Word of God or (the Bible) or (the Scriptures) for the remainder of our study.*

*So, if* <u>YOU</u> *can personally* **prove** *that the Word of God is just simply another book, and is* <u>not</u> *really the record of Truth . . . then you do not need to, and should not, listen to anything else that this author has to say.*

*However, if* <u>**YOU**</u> *cannot* <u>**disprove**</u> *the Word of God as being genuine, and from God . . . then* <u>**YOU**</u> *had better tune in, and listen to what is presented within this work.*

# The Creator God
# Creates A M.A.N.

As the Supreme Spirit Being of the Universe . . . and with the desire to produce an intimate family of His own . . . the Almighty Creator God purposes to create and bring forth a moral creature, that is as close to being like Himself as He possibly can.

> **"And God said, Let us make** *a* **man** *. . . a* **(<u>M</u>***anifested* **<u>A</u>***nimated* **<u>N</u>***eophyte)* **in our** *own interior* **image,** *and* **after our** *own exterior* **likeness: and let** *all of* **them have** *authoritative* **dominion over** *all of* **the fish of the sea, and over** *all of* **the fowl of the air, and over** *all of* **the cattle** *of the field***, and over all** *of* **the earth, and over every creeping thing that creepeth upon the earth."**
> *(Genesis 1:26; Enhanced)*

This new creature is a unique *species* of creation, and shall be labeled as **THE HUMAN BEING**.

**M**anifested **A**nimated **N**eophyte *(Meaning a New, Actively Revealed, Creation of Life)* is a proposed acronym for the MAN portion of the **HU-MAN BEING** that makes up the totality of the Hu**MAN**ity constituency of **MAN**kind.

This *species* of creation is an *Express Image* of God's own Personage . . . *(Hebrews 1:3)* carrying all of the qualities and aspects of the totality of God's Being, except for the *non-transferables* . . . which are Omniscience, Omnipotence, Omnipresence, and Self-Existence from everlasting. These non-transferable qualities belong only to the Personage of God, and to God alone, and could not be transferred unto Adam even if God desired to.

This *species* of creature is designed to be the ***Superior Species*** of all of creation . . . with only the Creator Himself holding a higher position. *(I Corinthians 15:27; Hebrews 2:8)*

This *species* of creature has been placed in a position of responsibility and authority that extends to the perimeters of this universe. *(Genesis 1:26; Psalms 8:4-6; Hebrews 2:8)*

The first individual of this *species* of creation, named Adam, is ***of*** God and belongs ***to*** God, by reason of direct creation. Legal ties are in place and God and His M.A.N. are connected. God is responsible for him.

This *species* of creature is destined for glory.

# DESTRUCTION AND DEATH
## STRIKES <u>ALL</u>
# HUMAN BEINGS

*"But of the forbidden fruit of the* **Tree of the Knowledge of God and Evil, thou shalt not eat of it: for in the day that thou eatest thereof thou shalt surely die** *spiritually." (Genesis 2:17; Enhanced)*

   *"***Wherefore, as by one** *Human* **man** *named Adam,* **sin entered** *again for a second time back* **into the world, and** *the workings of spiritual and physical* **death** *began operating again* **by** *that* **sin: and so** *spiritual* **death passed upon all men, for that all have sinned** *and come short of the glory of God." (Romans 5:12; Enhanced)*

   The first M.A.N., a HUMAN BEING named Adam, knowingly, willingly, and consciously disobeyed God's orientation-directive to avoid the eating of the forbidden fruit of the Tree of the Knowledge of Good and Evil . . . and he originally sinned in doing so. *(Genesis 2:17; I Timothy 2:14)*
   The first M.A.N., a HUMAN BEING named Adam, condemned himself and his entire progeny to Spiritual Death, and a total loss of a full $1/3^{rd}$ of their

operating personal construct through his actions. *(Genesis 2:17; Romans 5:12)*

The HUMAN BEING named Adam has now become only soulishly and physically alive . . . but he is Spiritually Dead. *(Genesis 2:7; 2:17)* The spirit portion of his being, which is the primary $^1/_3$rd portion of his whole operating personage, is now void of the *Life* of God and is considered Spiritually Dead legally. The spirit itself does still exist, but it is empty and deflated.

All of Adam's children, and his children's children ad infinitum, which will extend unto the entire race of HUMAN BEING populous, are now Spiritually Dead as well . . . but soulishly and physically very much alive. *(Romans 3:23; 5:12)*

The spirit of **every** HUMAN BEING is now in need of a mandatory *New Birthing* unto Life, in order to be restored unto the original condition of creation purpose. *(John 3:3, 5)*

Through his actions, the HUMAN BEING named Adam permanently breaks, any and all of, the legal connections that he may have had with the living God.

The HUMAN BEING named Adam was God's representative agent for righteousness on this Earth, and he has defected from his position and responsibility through disobedience. *(Genesis 3:22-23)*

God no longer has a righteous HUMAN BEING agent here on the planet named Earth.

God is on the outside of planetary authority and operation, and looking in. He is under covenant privilege and obligation to no one.

Physical reproduction of Mankind begins to take place as HUMAN BEINGS proceed to **"replenish the earth"** according to God's direction. *(Genesis 1:28)*

* * *

# SCRIPTURALLY SPEAKING . . . HUMAN BEINGS ARE CALLED
# GENTILES

**"By these were the isles of the Gentiles divided into their own lands; every one after his own tongue, and after their own families, and within their own nations."** *(Genesis 10:5; Enhanced)*

This is the first use of the Biblical term . . . Gentile. A Gentile is the very *First* of *Three Kinds* of **HUMAN BEINGS** that shall come forth and dwell forever upon the Earth.

By way of a definition:

*A Gentile is a Kind of HUMAN BEING that is Spiritually Dead in their sins and missing a full $1/3^{rd}$ of their personal operating construct; and does not have any legal rights or connections with the God of all creation.* *(Ephesians 2:12)*

A Gentile-*Kind* of HUMAN BEING is indeed a two-dimensional thinking creature that is lacking in genuine spiritual insight, because of possessing a dead spirit.

A two-dimensional thinking Gentile is a *Kind* of HUMAN BEING that is capable of being religious, but not of really being spiritual, regardless of what they may think or say to the contrary.

Gentile-*Kind* of HUMAN BEINGS increased in numbers exponentially on this planet named Earth and waded deeply into wickedness and sin. *(Genesis 6:5)*

All HUMAN BEINGS on the face of this planet Earth from the time of the M.A.N. named Adam until the time of the M.A.N. named Abram were a Gentile-*Kind* of HUMAN BEING.

Adam was a Gentile-*Kind* of HUMAN BEING . . .
Abel was a Gentile-*Kind* of HUMAN BEING . . .
Cain was a Gentile-*Kind* of HUMAN BEING . . .
Seth was a Gentile-*Kind* of HUMAN BEING . . .
Enoch was a Gentile-*Kind* of HUMAN BEING . . .
Methuselah was a Gentile-*Kind* of HUMAN BEING . . .
Lamech was a Gentile-*Kind* of HUMAN BEING . . .
Noah was a Gentile-*Kind* of HUMAN BEING . . .
Japheth was a Gentile-*Kind* of HUMAN BEING . . .
Shem was a Gentile-*Kind* of HUMAN BEING . . .
Ham was a Gentile-*Kind* of HUMAN BEING . . .
Terah was a Gentile-*Kind* of HUMAN BEING . . .
and Abram was a Gentile-*Kind* of HUMAN BEING.

But even as a Gentile-*Kind*, one can readily see that they were all still **HUMAN BEINGS**.

Because of the reality of separation from the *Spiritual Life* that comes from God, the **Human Being** creation has fallen to a state of Existence Without *Life* Legalities. Scripturally speaking they were in a condition of ***"having no hope, and without God in the world."*** *(Ephesians 2:12b)*

At His discretion, God is able to approach and deal with any particular **Human Being** that He would choose. However, if God is going to redeem the whole of His finest creation endeavors, He is going to have to establish certain legal parameters within which to work.

\* \* \*

# SCRIPTURALLY SPEAKING . . . SOME HUMAN BEINGS ARE NOW CALLED HEBREWS

***"And there came one that had escaped*** *from the fray of battle,* **and told Abram the Hebrew; for he dwelt in the plain of Mamre the Amorite,** *who was the* **brother of Eshcol,** *and also the* **brother of Aner: and**

*these men* **were confederate** *with, and in league* **with Abram."** *(Genesis 14:13; Enhanced)*

## SOMETHING SIGNIFICANT HAS NOW HAPPENED!!

This is the first use of the Biblical term . . . Hebrew. A Hebrew is the *Second* of *Three Kinds* of **HUMAN BEINGS** that will come forth to forever inhabit this planet named Earth.

By way of a definition:

*A Hebrew (also called an Israelite; or called a Jew; or called "the Circumcision") is a Kind of HUMAN BEING that is Spiritually Dead in their sins and missing a full $^1/_3{}^{rd}$ of their personal operating construct . . . however, they are in a Blood-Covenant relationship with the God of all creation through an agreement that was struck between the living God . . . and a HUMAN BEING named Abram . . . who had his named changed to Abraham.* *(Genesis 15:5-15)*

The legal contract that has made such a tremendous difference between being a Gentile-*Kind* of HUMAN BEING, and being a Hebrew-*Kind* of HUMAN BEING, can be found in the Book of Genesis, within the context of Chapter 15.

**Hebrew-*Kinds*** of HUMAN BEINGS have established legal rights and connections with the God of all creation through the power of a fallible Blood-Covenant bond.

A **Hebrew** is still a two-dimensional thinking ***Kind*** of HUMAN BEING, that is lacking in genuine spiritual insight because of still possessing a dead spirit.

A **Hebrew** is still a two-dimensional thinking ***Kind*** of HUMAN BEING who does indeed have a validly established religion *(which is a designated set of rules and regulations by which he may contact and then have dealings with the living God)*, but **Hebrews** are not really spiritual, they are carnal or worldly, regardless of what they may think or say.

The first **Hebrew-*Kind*** of HUMAN BEING was originally the **Gentile-*Kind*** of HUMAN BEING named Abram.

A fallible Blood-Covenant bond *changed* Abram's name and his ***Kind*** of HUMAN BEING status. *(Genesis 17:5)*

Now, there are ***Two*** out of the ***Three Kinds*** of HUMAN BEINGS that shall forever be in existence, living on the planet Earth . . . the **Gentile-*Kind*** of HUMAN BEING and the **Hebrew-*Kind*** of HUMAN BEING . . . also called a Jew.

Abram, the **Gentile-*Kind*** of HUMAN BEING became Abraham, a **Hebrew-*Kind*** of HUMAN

BEING, because of the Blood-Covenant bond that was established with the Creator God.

Sarai, his Gentile-*Kind* of HUMAN BEING wife, became Sarah, a **Hebrew-*Kind*** of HUMAN BEING, because of her Blood-Covenant marriage to Abraham.

Isaac, their divinely promised son, was actually born as a **Hebrew-*Kind*** of HUMAN BEING. *(Genesis 17:19)*

Jacob, their divinely purpose-of-election grandson, was also born as a **Hebrew-*Kind*** of HUMAN BEING. *(Romans 9:11)*

Jacob's twelve sons, Reuben, Simeon, Levi, Judah, Dan, Naphtali, Gad, Asher, Issachar, Zebulon, Joseph, and Benjamin, were all born as **Hebrew-*Kind*** of HUMAN BEINGS.

Thus, the entire HUMAN BEING Nation of Israel was created and developed by the Creator God that there might now be a Blood-Covenant bond *Kind* of HUMAN BEING upon the Earth, that the Creator God could have righteous representation agency and dealings with.

\* \* \*

# BRING FORTH A
# REDEEMER FROM
# THIS BLOOD-BOND *KIND* OF
# HUMAN BEING

*"For God so loved the whole world, that he gave his only begotten Son, that upon his resurrection from the dead, whosoever believeth in him should not perish, but have everlasting life."* (John 3:16; Enhanced)

*"But when the fulness of the time was finally come, God sent forth his Son Jesus, who was made of a Human woman, and was made under the conditions and restrictions of the Law of Moses,*

*To originally redeem them that were under the law of Moses, that we might receive the adoption of sons."* (Galatians 4:4-5; Enhanced)

The Creator God once again, through the **Hebrew-*Kind*** of a M.A.N. named Abraham, has righteous representation agency in the Earth utilizing the new Blood-Covenant bond *(The Abrahamic Blood Covenant)* that is established with the **Hebrew-*Kind*** of HUMAN BEINGS. *(Genesis 15:6)*

This presents the Creator God with a platform from which He is able to provide a HUMAN BEING *Redeemer* for any and all of the different _Kinds_ of HUMAN BEINGS who would desire to obey and follow Him . . . beginning, of course, with the Hebrew-*Kind* of HUMAN BEING belonging to the Nation of Israel. *(Galatians 4:5)*

\* \* \*

## THE NECESSITY OF PRECEDENT AND THE LEGALITIES OF A NEEDED SACRIFICE

### *Step #1*
### *"Unto Adam also and to his wife did the Lord God make coats of skins, and clothed them." (Genesis 3:21)*

Sacrifice . . . specifically animal sacrifice, began within the Garden of Eden. Adam and Eve had disobeyed God and attempted to clothe themselves with leaves when they knew that they were bodily naked, and became ashamed. *(Genesis 3:7)*

Before God dismissed them from the locale where the Tree of Life was resident, God instructed them concerning the details of animal sacrifice. When the instruction was complete, God utilized the remaining skins of the animals to fashion *"coats of skins"* for protection and warmth. *(Genesis 3:21)*

This particular, original sacrifice was for the purpose of instruction for HUMAN BEINGS, and the establishing of a necessary and mandatory ordinance of a periodic offering of *Sacrifice* . . . which is substantiated when we observe the sacrifice obligations of Cain and Abel. *(Genesis 4:3-4)*

It was not a Sin offering sacrifice, nor a sacrifice of acknowledgment, thanksgiving, and honor . . . it was instructional.

\* \* \*

## *Step #2*

**"And he said, Take now thy son, thine only son Isaac, whom thou lovest, and get thee into the land of Moriah; and offer him there for a burnt offering upon one of the mountains which I will tell thee of.** *(Genesis 22:2)*

**"And Abraham took the wood of the burnt offering, and laid it upon Isaac his son; and he took the fire in his hand, and a knife, and they went both of them together.**

**And Isaac spake unto Abraham his father, and said, My father: and he said, Here am I, my son. And he said, Behold the fire and the wood: but where is the lamb for a burnt offering?**

**And Abraham said, My son, God will provide himself a lamb for a burnt offering: so they went both of them together."** *(Genesis 22:6-8)*

We are now approximately 2,000 years down the road with Mankind. There have been a few animal sacrifices along the way, but they would not be sacrifices for Sin, as there is no given Law of Moses that is in place as yet, and no law-breaking that has occurred. And, Sin is not imputed where there is no law. *(Romans 5:13)*

There is, at present, an established Blood-Covenant bond that is in place. The Abrahamic Blood Covenant has been instituted between the Gentile-*Kind* . . . turned Hebrew-*Kind* *(because of the Blood-Covenant)* . . . a man named Abraham *(Genesis 14:13)* and the living God.

The Law of Moses is still approximately four-hundred years distant in the future. So this sacrifice that we are looking at in the above verses is not going to be a sacrifice for Sin, but a precedent setting, prophetic sacrifice, in preparation for the *final* sacrifice of the *Lamb of God*, who will ultimately be the Lord Jesus Christ of Nazareth.

\* \* \*

### Step #3

**"And they said, The God of the Hebrews hath met with us: let us go, we pray thee, three days' journey into the desert, and sacrifice unto the Lord our God; lest he fall upon us with pestilence, or with the sword."** *(Exodus 5:3)*

Even though Moses is the one who is speaking unto the Pharaoh in this verse, the actual Law of Moses has not yet been given unto the Hebrew-*Kind* of people . . . so this sacrifice that is being referenced above concerns the mandatory obligation of *Sacrifice* that was originally instituted by God within the Garden of Eden.

Within the *Bible-Time-Frame* there is now a Nation of Chosen People of God, who because of their continuing connection with God, adhere to the verbal *passed-on-down-the-road* instructions that will later be mandated within the written Word of God when it is penned.

A series of steps are being laid for the purpose of ultimately dealing with the heinous Law of Sin once and for all. Legalities must be established for this to hold fast on a universal level. The Proper order of execution must be adhered to, and no short-cuts will be acceptable.

\* \* \*

### Step #4

**"Then Moses called for all the elders of Israel, and said unto them, Draw out and take you a lamb according to your families, and kill the Passover."** *(Exodus 12:21)*

**"And ye shall observe this thing for an ordinance to thee and to thy sons for ever.**

**And it shall come to pass, when ye be come to the land which the Lord will give you, according as he hath promised, that ye shall keep this service.**

*And it shall come to pass, when your children shall say unto you, What mean ye by this service?*

*That ye shall say, It is the sacrifice of the Lord's Passover, who passed over the houses of the children of Israel in Egypt, when he smote the Egyptians, and delivered our houses. And the people bowed the head and worshipped."* (Exodus 12:24-27)

This obligatory sacrifice of the Passover Lamb shall be the last honor ordinance-type of sacrifice before the issuance of the Law of Moses. Further nuances are indeed involved in this sacrifice. However, none of them really have anything to do with the Sin problem directly, and they are all prophetic.

\* \* \*

### Step #5

*"And the Lord said unto Moses, Thus thou shalt say unto the children of Israel, Ye have seen that I have talked with you from heaven.*

*Ye shall not make with me gods of silver, neither shall ye make unto you gods of gold.*

*An altar of earth thou shalt make unto me, and shalt sacrifice thereon thy burnt offerings and thy peace offerings, thy sheep, and thine oxen: in all places where I record my name I will come unto thee, and I will bless thee.*

*And if thou wilt make me an altar of stone, thou shalt not build it of hewn stone: for if thou lift up thy tool upon it, thou hast polluted it.*

*Neither shalt thou go up by steps unto mine altar, that thy nakedness be not discovered thereon."* *(Exodus 20:22-26)*

We have now arrived at Exodus chapter 20 where the Ten Commandments are given by God through the M.A.N. named Moses, to the Hebrew-*Kind* of people, who are the children of the Nation of Israel, for the purpose of their behavior modification. And this discourse would be the prelude to the innocent animal, sacrificial system, *repair kit*, which was installed by God to preserve the life of any Hebrew-*Kind* of HUMAN BEING that breaks the Law of Moses in any way.

## RETURN TO THE REDEEMER

Jesus Christ of Nazareth is a Hebrew-*Kind* of HUMAN BEING.

His Terrestrial body was prepared, by utilizing a young, Hebrew-*Kind* of HUMAN BEING virgin girl, who was overshadowed by the power of the Creator God, *(Luke 1:35)* and she conceived supernaturally within her womb. *(Hebrews 10:5)*

Upon that miraculous occurrence, the Second Person of the Godhead, titled The Word, stepped into that conceived ovum, wrapped that Terrestrial body around Himself, and incarnated into the Hebrew-*Kind* of HUMAN BEING, God/M.A.N., named Jesus Christ of Nazareth.

Jesus of Nazareth grew up as a Hebrew-*Kind* of HUMAN BEING, under the operating conditions of the Law of Moses . . . *(The Ten Commandments, and the Feasts of the Lord, and the Sabbath of Commandment, and necessary Circumcision, and the Eating Regulations, and various other nuances)* . . . which were put into place, concerning ***only*** the Hebrew-*Kind*, Chosen People of God, HUMAN BEINGS, because of transgressions. *(Galatians 3:19)*

Contrary to the declarations of Spiritually-Dead men, when he became an adult Hebrew-*Kind* of HUMAN BEING, Jesus of Nazareth fulfilled all of the *Mosaic Law* requirements flawlessly. *(Matthew 5:17)*

At a point in time, the adult Hebrew-*Kind* of HUMAN BEING, named Jesus of Nazareth was captured by the other adult Hebrew-*Kind* of HUMAN BEINGS that were in the city of Jerusalem, and subsequently put to death.

On the cross of Calvary, the Law of Sin ***Spiritually*** *murdered* the Hebrew-*Kind* of HUMAN BEING named Jesus of Nazareth . . . and collectively, both the adult, Gentile-*Kind* and the Hebrew-*Kind* of HUMAN BEINGS, working together, ***Physically*** *murdered* the Terrestrial, physical body of the **Hebrew-*Kind*** of HUMAN BEING named Jesus of Nazareth.

When Universal, Spiritual, Sin indebtedness was totally satisfied, the Creator God *Birthed* the *murdered spirit* of the **Hebrew-*Kind*** of HUMAN BEING named Jesus of Nazareth, back into a new *Spiritual-Life* **PROTOTYPE-*Kind*** of HUMAN BEING called a **New Creature**. *(II Samuel 7:14; Psalms 2:7; Acts 13:33)*

Moreover, the *murdered* Terrestrial, physical body of the **Hebrew-*Kind*** of HUMAN BEING named Jesus of Nazareth was <u>*Resurrected*</u> back unto *Physical-Life* once again. *(Acts 13:33)*

When that event actually occurred, the *Third* of the ***Three Kinds*** of HUMAN BEINGS that shall dwell upon this Earth always was brought forth, and that ***Kind*** of a HUMAN BEING is now called a **New Creation-*Kind*** of HUMAN BEING.

The **Hebrew-*Kind*** of HUMAN BEING named Jesus of Nazareth <u>CHANGED</u> his HUMAN BEING ***KIND*** of status because of the ratification of a New Blood Covenant, *(Hebrews 8:7; 10:9)* and he is no longer viably in existence. *(II Corinthians 5:16)*

This same Jesus of Nazareth person has now become the very *First* **New Creation-*Kind*** of HUMAN BEING.

\* \* \*

# SCRIPTURALLY SPEAKING . . . SOME HUMAN BEINGS ARE NOW CALLED
# NEW CREATURES

*"**Therefore if any man** or woman **be** found abiding **in Christ, he is a** brand New Creature: all **old things** of his former life **are passed away; behold, all things** within his existence **are** now **become** brand **new."***
*(II Corinthians 5:17; Enhanced)*

All ***Three Kinds*** of HUMAN BEINGS that shall forever be in existence are now manifesting on this Earth, in this very day and hour.

*"**For as many of you as have been baptized into** the Spiritual Death of **Christ** Jesus **have put on Christ.***
*Where **there is** <u>neither</u> Jew **nor** Gentile **Greek. There is neither bond nor free. There is neither male nor female** anymore: **for ye are all one in Christ Jesus"*** *(Galatians 3:27-28; Enhanced)*

*"**And have put on the** New **man, which is re-newed in** revelation **knowledge after the** very **image of him that created him.***

*Where there is <u>neither</u> Gentile **Greek nor Jew** anymore. There is neither **circumcision nor uncircumcision,** nor **Barbarian, Scythian, bond nor free: but Christ is all and in all.** " (Colossians 3:10-11; Enhanced)*

Even concerning the Personage of Christ Jesus himself . . .

*"**Wherefore** because of these things, **henceforth**, from this time forth, **know we no man after the flesh** anymore: **yea, though we have known** Christ after the flesh when he walked upon this Earth as a **Hebrew-Kind** of person, **yet now henceforth,** from the time of his resurrection, know we him no more the same way that we once knew him, because he is a **New Creation.** " (II Corinthians 5:16; Enhanced)*

By way of a definition:

Any Gentile-*Kind* of HUMAN BEING that accepts what Jesus Christ of Nazareth has accomplished within the finished work of the cross of Calvary . . . and becomes **Born-Again** within their spirit . . . automatically becomes a New Creation-*Kind* of HUMAN BEING. They are no longer a Gentile-*Kind* of HUMAN BEING . . . because they are brand New. *(II Corinthians 5:17-18)*

Any Hebrew-*Kind* of HUMAN BEING that accepts what Jesus Christ of Nazareth has accomplished within the finished work of the cross of Calvary . . . and becomes **Born-Again** within their spirit . . .

automatically becomes a New Creation-*Kind* of HU-
MAN BEING. They are no longer a Hebrew-*Kind* of
HUMAN BEING . . . because they are brand New. *(II Corinthians 5:17-18)*

God does not make any *Hybrid*-**Kind** of
HUMAN BEINGS . . . ever . . . so—

Concerning all previous Hebrew-*Kind* of HU-
MAN BEINGS—

The term, *Messianic-Jew*, is not a Biblically sound,
Scriptural term, nor a spiritual reality. It is an attempt
by Biblically unknowledgeable men to foist the idea
upon Christendom that a previous Hebrew-*Kind* of
HUMAN BEING is now a half-Hebrew and half-
New Creation-*Kind* of HUMAN BEING. There is
no such thing in existence.

The term, *Completed-Jew*, is not a Biblically sound,
Scriptural term, nor a spiritual reality. It is an attempt
by Biblically unknowledgeable men to foist the idea
upon Christendom that a previous Hebrew-*Kind* of
HUMAN BEING is now a half-Hebrew and half-
New Creation-*Kind* of a HUMAN BEING. There is
no such thing in existence.

Previous Gentile-*Kind* of HUMAN BEINGS do
not seem to have any problem in this area.

The NEW CREATION reality that is extensively
taught within the writings of the Apostle Paul is, sad to

say, largely unrecognized and grossly under-taught within modern-day Christendom. However, that does not change spiritual reality or truth.

There are today **THREE KINDS** of HUMAN BEINGS in existence, on this planet Earth. The GENTILE-*Kind* of HUMAN BEING, and the HEBREW-*Kind* of HUMAN BEING, and the NEW CREATION-*Kind* of HUMAN BEING. And none of them are *Hybrids*.

And what individual men may say, and try to put forth because of their own beliefs and convictions, does not change the Truth of the Word of God.

It is not the responsibility of declared Truth, to search out what we personally choose to believe, and then to line up with us.

It is our personal responsibility, to find out what the declared Truth is according to the Word of God, and then decide if we want to choose to line up with it or not.

\* \* \*

# CONCERNING THE DESTRUCTION:

If **<u>YOU</u>** are currently a Gentile-*Kind* of HUMAN BE-ING . . . *then YOU are Spiritually Dead in your sins and missing a full $^1/_3^{rd}$ of your personal operating construct; and you do not have any legal rights or connections with the God of all creation.* (Ephesians 2:12) Even if you profess that you believe in God . . . it does not really matter one bit. You are slated for everlasting Destruction when you physically die should you choose to remain the way that you are, because you are Spiritually Dead . . . and there are no Dead spirits being allowed in Heaven.

If **<u>YOU</u>** are currently a **Hebrew-*Kind*** of HUMAN BEING . . . *then YOU are Spiritually Dead in your sins and missing a full $^1/_3^{rd}$ of your personal operating construct; and even though you are in a Blood-Covenant relationship with the God of all creation, that Covenant has temporarily been suspended and a New Christian Blood-Covenant has now been established in its place.* (Hebrews 10:8-10) You need to make a decision to place your trust in the finished work of the cross of Calvary, and what Jesus of Nazareth has accomplished. Without being **Born-Again** within your spirit, you are still slated for everlasting Destruction when you physically die should you choose to remain the way that you are, because you are Spiritually Dead . . . and there are no Dead spirits being allowed in Heaven.

If **YOU** are currently a New Creation-*Kind* of HUMAN BEING . . . *then YOU are Spiritually Alive within your spirit and your sins have been forgiven. Your missing full $^1/_3^{rd}$ of your personal operating construct has been restored, and you are a participant of the New Christian Blood-Covenant that has been established because of the finished work of Jesus Christ of Nazareth upon the cross of Calvary.* You have been **Born-Again** within your spirit, and you are slated for everlasting, glorious, radiant *Spiritual Life*, forevermore. Living spirits are allowed in Heaven, and you are now *alive* because of your **New-Birth**.

# What will it take for HUMAN BEINGS to tune-in and listen to the Truth? Please . . . do not . . . PERISH!

# HOW TO
# NOT PERISH!

From the time of their physical birth **ALL** HUMAN BEINGS, including <u>**YOU**</u>, are Spiritually Dead in their sins, because of Adam's disobedience.
*(Romans 3:23; 5:12; 6:16)*

Jesus of Nazareth said that every HUMAN BEING *must* be ***Born-Again*** within their spirit. Our only part to play in the scenario of <u>not</u> perishing is to surrender to what Jesus says must take place . . . and that is all.

Pray this prayer out loud with me, and mean it from your heart.

*"**Dear Jesus,***

*I recognize that I am a sinner, and am not able to redeem myself, no matter what I do, so I need your help. You stated that every person must be Born-Again within their spirit to be released from the spiritual bondage that Human Beings are in, and the servitude that we experience from the powers of darkness.*

*In accordance to the declarations of the Word of God, I choose to believe that you were born of a virgin girl, and that you lived a sinless life, and that you ultimately allowed yourself to be taken by the powers of darkness and viciously tortured.*

*You were condemned to death on the cross of Calvary, and actually died in my sins because you did not have any. You were condemned to Hell in my place, and spent three days and three nights within the bowels of this Earth.*

*After three days you were raised up from the dead both spiritually and physically, and I was raised up with you.*

*I ask you to forgive me of all of my past sins totally, and cleanse me by your precious blood and make me brand new. I renounce Satan and all of the works of darkness, and pledge myself to serve you forever. I place my trust in you, and all that you have done for me. Thank you so very much.*

*From this moment on . . . I will declare that I am a child of the Most High God, and I will purpose to live my life for you from now on. I ask and declare these things in your blessed name, in the name of Jesus. Amen"*

Now that **YOU** are a New Creature *in Christ* you belong to a completely different spiritual Kingdom *(Colossians 1:13)* and do not have to obey the Devil any more but are allowed to operate according to a whole new set of spiritual laws.

Begin the *cleansing process* (*II Corinthians 7:1*) which is YOUR responsibility. Actively start *putting off the Old Man which is corrupt according to the deceitful lusts, and start putting on the New Man which is created in righteousness and true holiness.* (*Ephesians 4:22-24*) And *lay aside every weight and the sin which doth so easily beset us.* (*Hebrews 12:1*)

Find a Bible-believing church in your area and become an active member. Determine what Motivational Gifting you have been blessed with, according to Romans 12:6-8, and purpose to develop and utilize that gifting for the benefit of the Body of Christ.

Trust in God in all things, learn how to walk by faith, and purpose to be a blessing in whatever God will have you to do. The Lord bless you in all that you put your hand to.

Maranatha!

# *Meet the Author*

---

By-The-Book Ministries, Inc. began in 2001 as a teaching outreach. Rob E. Daley has been gifted by God to be able to explain biblical truths in an easy to understand manner.

Many have been blessed by his teaching style.

Rob was saved and filled with the Holy Spirit in 1978 and has been instructed by the greatest teacher of all—the Spirit of Truth Himself. Rob is an ordained minister with the Assemblies of God International Fellowship and has pastored in various churches over the past 34 years.

It is the desire of this ministry to see the body of Christ solidly taught, and grow up into the things of the Lord. Rob is available for seminars, retreats, conventions, etc.

Rob can be reached at:

thedaleys@bythebookministries.org

http://robdaleyauthor.com

www.ingramcontent.com/pod-product-compliance
Lightning Source LLC
LaVergne TN
LVHW010023070426
835508LV00001B/32